How to
Launch PLCs
in Your District

W. Richard Smith

Solution Tree | Press

555 North Morton Street
Bloomington, IN 47404
800.733.6786 (toll free) / 812.336.7700
FAX: 812.336.7790

email: info@solution-tree.com
solution-tree.com

Visit **go.solution-tree.com/PLCbooks** to download the reproducibles in this book.

Printed in the United States of America

19 18 17 16 15   1 2 3 4 5

Library of Congress Cataloging-in-Publication Data

Smith, W. Richard.
  How to launch PLCs in your district / by W. Richard Smith.
     pages cm. -- (Solutions)
  Includes bibliographical references.
  ISBN 978-1-936765-39-3 (perfect bound) 1. Professional learning communities--United States. 2. Teachers--In-service training. 3. Educational leadership--United States. I. Title.
  LB1731.S555 2015
  371.2'011--dc23
                              2015010058

Solution Tree
Jeffrey C. Jones, CEO
Edmund M. Ackerman, President

Solution Tree Press
President: Douglas M. Rife
Associate Acquisitions Editor: Kari Gillesse
Editorial Director: Lesley Bolton
Managing Production Editor: Caroline Weiss
Copy Chief: Sarah Payne-Mills
Copy Editor: Jessi Finn
Proofreader: Elisabeth Abrams
Text and Cover Designer: Rian Anderson
Compositor: Rachel Smith

Acknowledgments

Deepest appreciation to Tracy Smith, my wife, for her love and support.

Thank you also to Kathy Hushek, JoDee Marcellin, Cindy Toews, Sylvia Hill, Steve Carlson, Jim Simpson, Mandy Chacon, Dennis Wiechmann, Rosemary Sancho, and Jennifer Smith for their above-and-beyond efforts as we learned together and worked to transform a district.

Visit **go.solution-tree.com/PLCbooks** to download the reproducibles in this book.

Table of Contents

Chapter 3: Monitoring to Sustain Momentum **45**

Chapter 4: Ensuring Sustainability Through Ongoing Commitment and Implementation. **59**

References and Resources **67**

About the Author

 **W. Richard Smith** was deputy superintendent of the Sanger Unified School District, which serves more than ten thousand students with a large population of minority and high-poverty students. He has been involved in public education for more than thirty-three years. Smith has presented on the power of professional learning communities throughout California, and more than 160 districts statewide have visited Sanger to see its collaborative culture firsthand. Smith has taught at the elementary and high school levels and has served as a special education resource teacher. He was principal of four elementary schools and was a high school administrator for nine years. He also worked in the district office for ten years.

When Smith joined Sanger in 2004 as assistant superintendent for human resources, the district was one of ninety-eight in California to be named a program improvement district due to low performance among English learners. Two years later, Sanger became one of the first districts to rise above this status and is now one of the highest-performing districts in the Central Valley. Among all eighteen schools, Sanger has won multiple state and national awards, eleven California Distinguished School awards, eight Title I Academic Achievement awards, two nominations for National Blue Ribbon Schools, and one National Blue Ribbon School award.

Smith was named the 1998 Crystal Award Winner for the Clovis Unified School District for his leadership and work at the high school level. In 2010, he was named a distinguished alumnus by the Kremen School of Education and Human Development at California State University, Fresno. Additionally, California State University, Fresno, honored Smith as the 2014 Top Dog Distinguished Alumni Award winner.

To book W. Richard Smith for professional development, contact pd@solution-tree.com.

Introduction

One of the most insightful statements I have ever heard regarding school improvement is, "It has to be something that *ordinary* educators can do." This statement cuts to the crux of what is needed to launch professional learning communities (PLCs) on a districtwide basis. If we are to create PLCs across an entire school system, we must provide leadership, strategies, and tools so that ordinary educators can actually make it happen.

PLC implementation in the Sanger Unified School District, my school district, transformed what was ranked as one of California's ninety-eight worst school districts in 2004 to one of the state's most successful districts. Districtwide PLC implementation transformed teachers' and administrators' perspectives and work. A laser-like focus on ensuring student learning has led to consistent achievement gains since 2004 (Smith, 2012).

District educators collaborated to transform an entire school system serving a multilingual, low socioeconomic, and highly underrepresented population into a place where students learn and achieve at levels many thought were impossible. Professional learning communities became something that ordinary educators did to produce extraordinary achievement results. Our districtwide implementation did not happen by accident. It happened intentionally with an explicit focus on making implementation doable.

I've learned that to implement professional learning communities districtwide, we must be willing to measure and secure the district leaders' commitment. The odds for successful districtwide implementation plummet without the understanding, buy-in, and support of the district office; key district leaders—such as the superintendent and governing board—control and guide district direction, budgets, personnel resources, scheduling, communication, and political support.

A Focus on Commitment and Longevity

When district leaders commit to districtwide PLC implementation, they must base their decision on a clear understanding of what PLC implementation means and what it will take to make it happen. The decision to implement PLCs cannot be based on hasty agreements, such as the following.

- "Hey, District X did it, and it worked for them."
- "Let's try this to see if it works."
- "We already have meetings. Let's call them professional learning communities."

These abrupt decisions are recipes for disaster and make PLCs seem like a surefire solution.

Instead, a commitment to PLC implementation must be based on knowledge and facts. It requires leaders to make explicit and intentional decisions grounded in a firm understanding of all elements of a PLC. In my interviews with school leaders whose districts have successfully implemented PLCs districtwide, all leaders cite that learning the basics of PLCs is a foundational component in beginning the journey toward implementation.

Marcus Johnson, 2011 National Superintendent of the Year, describes the start of his district's PLC implementation process: "As district leaders, our first step was to go to a conference and hear Rick and Becky DuFour explain professional learning communities. Without that basic understanding, our efforts would not have been as focused and direct" (personal communication, March 21, 2009).

Similarly, Wesley Sever, Kingsburg Elementary Charter School District superintendent, notes, "I bought and read a copy of *Learning by Doing* [DuFour, DuFour, Eaker, & Many, 2010]. It became a pillar of my understanding of professional learning communities and gave me the tools to answer questions as we began the journey. By reading and learning, I had the tools to explain why this [professional learning community] work was important to our students and why we were committed to implementation" (personal communication, March 2, 2015).

To support their commitment to the PLC model, district leaders can begin to secure budgetary and personnel resources to ensure successful implementation. Their willingness to provide these resources in support of implementation is a clear measure of their commitment. Districts that broadcast their commitment but do not support implementation with resources create administrative mirages with no substance. Their PLC implementation is in name only.

Committing to PLC implementation cannot be a one-time event. The journey to implementation demands a long-term pledge. No place on this journey is *good enough*. Commitment to implementation must be a multiyear process that continually deepens understanding.

As district leader during Sanger Unified's first year of districtwide implementation, I met with principals and teachers and discussed their PLC implementation. To measure buy-in, I asked them, "Are your teams committed to implementing the PLC model at your school?" During one of these visits, a teacher turned to me and asked, "Are you truly committed to supporting our professional learning community work for more than this one year?"

Her question is burned into my mind. Without the district leadership's continuous explicit and intentional commitment to PLC implementation, PLCs could quickly look like a magic fix or a silver bullet. As district and school-site educators, we all have daily to-do lists made up of important tasks. To complete our to-do lists, time and energy are the most valuable resources we have available; when it comes to PLCs, many educators meet the prospect of investing time and energy into another improvement initiative with skepticism and cynicism. For instance, during a workshop, I asked the educators in the audience to list the school-improvement initiatives that their district had embarked on in the last five years. The educators, on average, listed ten initiatives. One of the attendees summed up what all the teachers felt regarding new initiatives, saying, "Give it time, and it will pass."

Commitment to too many initiatives stretches resources, focus, and buy-in. Schools and teachers have a finite capacity to implement multiple initiatives. The advent of too many initiatives also drains the critical resources of time and energy. Michael Fullan (2011) notes that effective districts identify a few key priorities and then "pursue them relentlessly" (p. 69). In pursuing districtwide PLC implementation, we must be willing to relentlessly commit to ensuring appropriate support. District leadership must take stock of the number of initiatives that are planned and measure them against school staff's capacity and the resources needed to support these initiatives. Leaders who commit to too many initiatives risk their credibility should the initiatives fail or simply disappear.

So many initiatives billed as silver bullets for improving learning come and go that new initiatives are greeted with a *wait and see if this survives* attitude. Naysayers, both teachers and administrators, begin a vocal barrage of distain for the new initiative while citing past failures. The curse of failed silver bullets haunts all new initiatives and must be countered.

Bumps in the Road to PLC Implementation

Targeted commitment is essential to successful PLC implementation, especially while working through naysayers' cynicism, occasional missteps, and the logistics of implementation. Realizing that bumps will occur during implementation should not cause fear but rather remind us that some struggles are necessary to implement a lasting improvement program.

Implementation is never as simple as one imagines. In his presentations, Luis Cruz (2013), a sought-after educator and speaker, notes two different versions of implementation: (1) imagined and (2) actual. See figure I.1 for a visual interpretation.

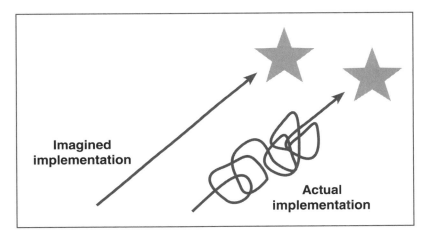

Figure I.1: Imagined and actual implementation.

Leaders with imagined implementation tend to get thrown when confronted with setbacks. Their commitment level remains high until obstacles appear. These leaders search for the silver bullet rather than taking time to truly commit. Two ways to deal with these setbacks are (1) facing your district in the right direction and (2) changing district culture.

Facing Your District in the Right Direction

Every school district wants to know how to become a system that produces high levels of learning for its students. In many districts, this results in constantly searching for a quick fix that will lead to greater student achievement. These districts continuously use terms such as *best practices*, *building capacity*, and *continuous improvement* without putting them into the context of a long-term plan that has direction and purpose. These districts' leadership teams also focus on what works based on popular educational trends rather than on their districts' current circumstances. These districts often have difficulty explaining why they have chosen to pursue a direction or program. To help sustain long-term change and to keep everyone on the same page, district leaders must present an argument for and a focus on collaboration. They must also adjust their district mission statement to be more pragmatic.

An Argument for and a Focus on Collaboration

Schools and districts beginning the journey toward building a PLC often find themselves searching for their first step and asking, "How do we get off to a good start so we create a movement that promotes buy-in and understanding?" Prior to taking the first step in any journey, one must face the right direction. Understanding the why of implementing a professional learning community is essential to building understanding and buy-in for those who will learn and work within the community.

Members of PLCs work to create and maintain (DuFour & Fullan, 2013):

- A relentless focus on learning for all students
- A collaborative culture and collective effort to support student and adult learning
- A results orientation to improve practice and drive continuous improvement

These core targets allow us to measure our development and ensure that we are facing the right direction.

Every prospective teacher interviewed at Dry Creek Elementary was asked, "Do you want to be the teacher with the highest student achievement at our school or a member of a team whose students all achieve at high levels?" The question focuses on the fundamental elements of developing a PLC. Prospective candidates signaled to the interview committee of teachers their willingness to share and learn together for all students' benefit. Candidates selected to teach at the school entered with a clear understanding that this community of professionals prioritized learning for all. All teachers at this site were responsible for student achievement.

Educational institutions, districts, schools, and teaching and administrative positions exist to ensure that all students learn. At the root of all district and school goals lies this fundamental purpose. The purpose is reflected through the haze of rambling mission statements convoluted by jargon. But with professional learning communities, this fundamental purpose becomes clear in well-written and clearly understood goals. These goals emphasize this purpose and set it at the heart of successful districtwide PLC implementation.

A Pragmatic Focus on Mission

Since the 1990s, school districts seeking what works have rushed to develop mission statements fueled by policy architects' zest for written documentation and a belief that these mission statements would transform education by moving to a business operation model. Districts have joined the movement by developing, adopting, posting, disseminating, and preaching mission statements as valuable tools with virtues clearly stating what schools aim to accomplish. Hundreds of staff hours and buckets of money were thrown into developing these mission statements to bring clarity and direction. Many districts frame their missions and proudly display them in their district offices.

During a leadership workshop I attended for superintendents and assistant superintendents, the attendees were asked whether their districts had developed and adopted district mission statements. Hands flew up around the room with virtually all participants indicating that their districts had such documents. Each attendee received a piece of paper with instructions to write his or her district's mission statement. A hush fell across the room. Suddenly, a participant raised his hand and asked, "We have one, but I can only vaguely tell you what it is. Should I write what I know?" His position in his district? Superintendent.

His paper contained the following statement: "To provide an environment with a technological focus to maximize student learning and ensure students are equipped to meet the challenges of the 21st century."

His district's actual mission statement read:

> [Name of district] seeks to create a challenging learning environment that encourages high expectations for success through development-appropriate instruction that allows for individual differences and learning styles. Our schools promote a safe, orderly, caring, and supportive environment. Each student's self-esteem is fostered by positive relationships with students and staff. We strive to have our parents, teachers, and community members actively involved in our students' learning.

A quick check revealed that of the forty-five attendees, none had been able to write his or her district's mission statement with any accuracy. It became clear to all the educators in attendance that they had mostly fallen back on jargon, a cadence of generic *educationalese* that bore little or no resemblance to what their districts had worked so diligently to create.

District leaders must share a common understanding of their district's fundamental purpose. Clearly stating what the district seeks to accomplish can best define this purpose. This must be done in pragmatic, clear, and simple terms that all members of the organization can comprehend and follow.

When I work with district leadership teams to clarify their fundamental purposes, I ask each member to write the district's top three goals on cards, one goal on each card, without discussion. We then lay the cards on a table and pair matching cards.

District leadership teams that do not have matching cards show little or no clarity of purpose. They do not speak with a common voice. In these districts, we often find random acts of improvement and multiple initiatives that show no continuity or unified purpose. Also, the schools and teachers in these districts are left baffled by what their districts strive to accomplish. Random acts of improvement lead to distrust of new initiatives and district leadership.

If the cards' messages are similar but do not match exactly, then it is incumbent on the leadership team to clarify and ensure a common voice. Districts led by a unified front tend to move cohesively until obstacles or challenges arise. Without a firm grasp on their purposes, districts meet new challenges with knee-jerk responses that may or may not provide solutions that propel them toward their vaguely understood overarching goals.

Districts with leadership teams that have clear purposes and goals will have cards that share common understandings. These districts can clearly articulate their goals and how they intend to meet these goals. When obstacles arise, these districts never lose sight of their focus as they formulate solutions, which provides schools, teachers, staff, and the community with a clear mission and a shared understanding of the district's direction.

I did the same card activity with a high-performing district known for ensuring learning for all students. The twelve district leadership team members were asked to write down and match up their overarching goals. All twelve team members had matching cards. Their district's purpose was clearly evidenced in the overarching goals they matched.

- Raise the achievement levels of all students.
- Close the achievement gap for all student subgroups.
- Maintain a safe, collaborative learning environment.

The district's overarching goals defined its fundamental purpose: to ensure that all students learn at high levels. No one in the organization was confused about the district's purpose or direction. Understanding what their district aimed to accomplish allowed these educators to build the supporting structures necessary to achieve these overarching goals.

Changing District Culture

Another bump in the road to PLC implementation is changing district culture. For example, a large urban school district hired a new superintendent, after the previous superintendent resigned and fled the district, to assemble a district leadership team to tackle the biggest impediment to district improvement—its toxic culture. When pressed on the toxic culture's root causes, the team of district leaders, principals, and teachers created the following list.

- Adult issues trump student learning.

- Teachers work in isolation with little buy-in to the district.

- There is a continual and ever-changing focus on staff development with every new initiative that the district attempts to implement.

- Principals have become school managers with little ownership.

- Compliance-driven requirements mandate the use of pacing guides and textbooks, regardless of whether students are learning from them.

- Required inspection and evaluation practices focus on finding problems rather than solving them.

This list represents the symptoms of a toxic culture but not the causal roots. The roots of a toxic culture grow from a lack of trust that blocks the formation of professional relationships, impedes the flow of necessary information, and corrupts a school district's identity. The successful implementation of the PLC model requires that we address district culture. A school district's culture forms the foundation on which to build successful PLC implementation.

About This Book

This book is intended to provide a comprehensive, but doable, approach to districtwide PLC implementation. I have sought to provide school and district leaders with a thorough guide with proven strategies. The design of this book focuses on four critical elements for successful implementation—with each of the following chapters focusing on an element. The four elements for successful districtwide PLC implementation are:

1. Developing a district guiding coalition and common language

2. Empowering site leadership through staff development and training

3. Monitoring to sustain momentum

4. Ensuring sustainability through ongoing commitment and implementation

Within each description of these four elements, I provide critical supporting strategies and considerations in detail. From forming a guiding coalition, developing a PLC vocabulary districtwide, and designing a staff development program to measuring growth and development, each chapter provides leaders with essential steps to follow on their implementation journey. I also provide practical, real-life examples of successful district implementation, as well as examples of pitfalls, from my own experiences working with schools and districts since 2005. In the instances of pitfalls, I have kept the names of participants and schools anonymous due to the confidential nature of the circumstances described.

Chapter 1

Developing a District Guiding Coalition and Common Language

District leaders' long-term commitment to pursuing PLCs solidifies implementation. Once district leaders confirm their long-term commitment, they can develop a guiding coalition. This coalition provides district leadership with an advisory group to guide, measure, and evaluate the district's implementation efforts.

"Forming a powerful guiding coalition starts with identifying the true leaders" in your district (Frampton et al., 2010, p. 56). This includes formal leaders—those in key power positions in the district—and informal leaders—those recognized for their leadership, credibility, and influence in all sites and departments:

> The guiding coalition (sometimes called a steering team . . .) includes representation from all key stakeholder groups . . . . It then grows over time as respected, reputable individuals with the capacity to lead from various sectors within the community are identified. Finding the right blend of strengths and interests pays great dividends toward future success. (Frampton et al., 2010, p. 56)

The highest-ranking individual responsible for PLC implementation should give the invitations to participate in a guiding coalition. In many cases, this may be the superintendent; in other cases, it may be a different leader charged with districtwide PLC implementation. The individual who hands out the invitations must ensure that invitees receive the training information they will need to fully understand PLCs, including a copy of *Learning by Doing* (DuFour et al., 2010), attendance to PLC institutes or workshops, and access to experts who can answer their technical questions. Those invited to become guiding coalition members must feel supported in developing their understanding.

The group's size should allow members to have constructive discussions—too large and the guiding coalition meetings become nothing more than informational gatherings; too small and the coalition may not give a realistic picture of the district's efforts.

District leaders must select members intentionally with a focus on ensuring successful implementation. Keep the following points in mind during your selection process.

- Consider those who have the following attributes within the district.
    - Credibility
    - Expertise
    - Influence
    - Position power
- Avoid inviting those who may see participation as a stepping-stone to getting administrative positions or gaining power.
- Invite those who listen well, give frank and honest observations, and have students' best interests at heart.
- Ensure that prospective members clearly understand the coalition's purpose.

Districts that form their guiding coalitions with individuals who seek to please district leadership rather than ensure successful implementation find themselves with unrealistic feedback. Often, these coalitions are labeled *yes committees* or *rubber stamps* for the administration because these individuals say exactly what they believe the administration wants to hear. Forming a guiding coalition that provides honest guidance and feedback is paramount, and careful member selection is the key. An effective, well-balanced guiding coalition provides a comprehensive picture of implementation through multiple perspectives. It focuses on offering multiple solutions and ideas that are essential to successful implementation.

As PLC implementation develops and the guiding coalition's understanding matures, the district can add additional members to the group. Attention should be paid to "maintain an appropriate balance of those with experience on the coalition and those who will infuse fresh perspectives" in expanding the guiding coalition (Frampton et al., 2010, p. 57).

Once you've chosen your group members, the coalition must fully prepare itself for implementation. For instance, it must develop a common understanding of end goals and vocabulary and must understand the structure of a PLC and the various implementation models in order to move forward efficiently.

Developing a Common Understanding

After establishing your guiding coalition, it is time to become a productive group. This begins with clearly defining the PLC implementation process, providing opportunities and materials to learn about PLCs, and developing a doable calendar of meetings that respects the members' time.

As part of the learning process, the guiding coalition should develop a set of norms to bring focus and direction to meetings and clarify professional relationships between members. (See *Learning by Doing* [DuFour et al., 2010] for more on building norms.) The guiding coalition must clearly understand its purpose and role. Meetings must have clearly targeted agendas leading to meaningful outcomes designed to support and ensure successful implementation. Meetings must allow time to discuss, share, ask questions, and find solutions to obstacles.

In addition, district leadership and the guiding coalition that leads districtwide PLC implementation must have a common framework in which to work and lead. They must share the same basic understanding and a common language of PLC implementation and its essential processes. "Language itself, then, is a critical tool for successful collaboration . . . [and] one of the keys to collaboration among educators, along with mutual respect and flexibility" (Ehren, Laster, & Watts-Taffe, 2009). It's tempting to think that one can easily lead district movements through a generalized view of the PLC implementation process. "Just develop a shared vision, and the rest will fall into place," we hear often. However, "for collaboration to be successful participants in the process have to create shared language for communication" (Ehren et al., 2009). But how can parties develop a shared vision when they have their own biases surrounding PLCs and don't have similar views of reality or the same expectations of the future?

A common language is essential. Without intentional focus, however, language can interfere with districtwide implementation. Teachers across disciplines and grade levels do not always use the same language, nor are they always aware of how other teachers use words because teachers may not converse much outside of their grade levels, departments, or schools. They understand their own vocabulary terms and working environments and may not know what vocabulary that teachers in different disciplines, grade levels, or schools use. Without shared meaning, educators may not be able to engage successfully in problem solving and decision making as they work toward implementation (Ehren et al., 2009).

Districts that have had success in developing common languages and frameworks have begun by reading and studying the critical questions and elements of the PLC process. See figure 1.1.

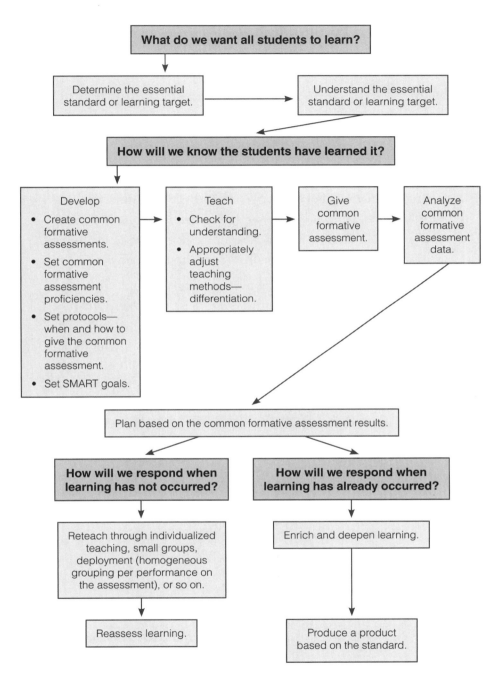

Figure 1.1: District PLC flowchart for common understanding.

But studying this flowchart and its elements is not enough. Translating the learned material into a doable, clear process with a common district language forms the nexus between learning and implementing.

This process begins with developing a district glossary of PLC terms that focuses on providing a common vernacular. The guiding coalition can play a major role in developing this glossary as the members read and learn. Guiding coalition members can highlight and record key vocabulary and terms necessary to understanding the PLC model and its processes as they read *Learning by Doing* (DuFour et al., 2010). With each term, they can provide a working definition that educators in the district will find meaningful.

During an early meeting, the guiding coalition compiles its vocabulary list with its working definitions. During this compilation process, guiding coalition members will see patterns of importance. Key vocabulary and terms will stand out and take on common meanings as the coalition members come to shared understandings. In most cases, the glossary created during this process ranges from twenty-five to thirty key terms. The following terms are some of the more common words found in these glossaries.

- Collaboration
- Collaborative teams
- Collective commitment
- Common formative assessment
- Essential learning
- Four critical questions of a PLC (see figure 1.1, page 17)
- Goals
- Interventions

- Learning data
- Mission
- Norms
- Protocol
- Reciprocal accountability
- Results orientation
- SMART goals
- Summative assessment
- Values
- Vision

Creating a glossary is a major step toward reaching a coherent PLC process, but it is only one step forward. Translating the PLC concept, vocabulary, and glossary of terms into doable actions requires a picture of the PLC process—a road map. The road map will guide others as they work through the PLC process.

A Road Map

After reading PLC materials, attending a PLC institute, and working to develop a district glossary, one of my guiding coalition members asked me, "This is great, but what steps do collaborative teams actually take when they meet?" The question pointed out a major need: guiding coalitions need a road map of actions—a personalized black-and-white map to guide their initial work.

Our guiding coalition had to make the work comprehendible to all members before expanding to district implementation. We needed to develop an *archetype*—"the original pattern or model from which all things of the same kind are copied or on which they are based; a model or first form; prototype" (Archetype, n.d.)—to guide our process. This archetype would create common understanding and consistent implementation across the district.

The guiding coalition was charged with defining the steps that school teams would go through in their work within a PLC. Because the guiding coalition had influential practitioners who understood PLC concepts and processes, as well as our schools' workings, they were instrumental in defining the steps necessary to ensure districtwide understanding and implementation. The guiding coalition started with a whiteboard and markers to create a flowchart for teams to follow.

As the guiding coalition talked through the PLC process and laid out teams' steps, a deeper understanding of purpose, relevance, and technical processes was revealed. The guiding coalition quickly realized that all teacher teams—from a kindergarten team to a high school algebra 1 team—need a clear pathway and common language for the PLC process. Ensuring that a team's steps are clear and sequential makes the process doable for everyone. See figure 1.2 for the guiding coalition's road map.

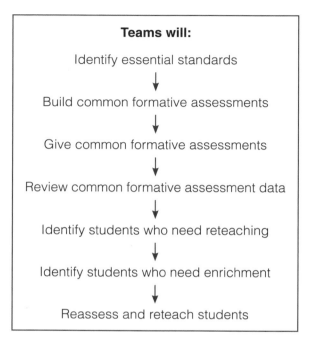

Teams will:

Identify essential standards

↓

Build common formative assessments

↓

Give common formative assessments

↓

Review common formative assessment data

↓

Identify students who need reteaching

↓

Identify students who need enrichment

↓

Reassess and reteach students

Figure 1.2: PLC road map.

The rudimentary road map in figure 1.2 provided a focal point for the guiding coalition's common understanding of districtwide PLC implementation. It also acted as a stepping-stone for refinement as the guiding coalition's work turned from understanding districtwide PLC implementation to actually implementing it.

The Eighteen Critical Issues

Prior to rolling out a districtwide staff development program that follows a PLC road map, the guiding coalition must fully understand eighteen critical issues that impact practice. Understanding and addressing these issues are necessary to ensure the development of a comprehensive staff development program that leads to implementation across all sites. The critical issues are as follows (DuFour et al., 2010).

1. Teams have identified norms and protocols to guide teamwork.

2. Teams analyze student data and establish SMART goals to improve achievement levels and ensure interdependence.

3. All team members clearly grasp the essential learning (knowledge, skills, and dispositions) that students must acquire in a grade level, course, or unit of study.

4. The study of essential learning aligns with state and district standards and high-stakes assessments required of students.

5. Teams identify content and topics that can be eliminated or reduced. They establish a focus on what is essential.

6. All team members reach an agreement on how to best sequence a course's content, and they set pacing guides to ensure understanding of essential learning.

7. Prerequisite knowledge and skills have been identified for all essential learning.

8. Instruments and strategies have been established to assess and screen students for prerequisite knowledge and skills.

9. Teams set up a system and strategies that assist students in acquiring prerequisite knowledge and skills when deficits surface. Basic response to intervention elements are in place.

10. Frequent common formative assessments help determine student mastery of essential learning.

11. Teams establish proficiency standards for skills and concepts on common formative assessments.

12. Common formative assessments' results are analyzed, and they build on students' strengths and address their

weaknesses as part of a continuous improvement cycle that ensures greater student learning.

13.   The results of common formative assessments help to identify students who need additional time and support to master essential learning. School systems and processes ensure that students receive this support in a timely manner.

14.   All team members, as well as students, clearly understand the criteria that judge the quality of students' work related to essential learning. The teams systematically calibrate the criteria to ensure that they consistently apply them in assessing student performance.

15.   Students know and understand the criteria they can use to self-assess the quality of their work. Students receive clear rubrics and examples of quality levels.

16.   Teachers develop common summative assessments and use them to assess programs' strengths and weaknesses.

17.   Common summative assessments explicitly state and present proficiency standards for skills and concepts to measure student learning.

18.   Teams establish a formal evaluation of adherence to team norms, the effectiveness of teams, and adherence to the defined PLC process.

Addressing each issue is necessary for successful PLC implementation. The guiding coalition must gain an understanding and appreciation for each issue's importance in order to assist in designing, reviewing, and monitoring training and implementation.

Leaving out these issues greatly diminishes the viability of a PLC. For example, in my district's initial implementation and training, we believed that teaching teams to develop shared norms was not necessary. We thought teams would function just fine without *wasting* time on training that would ensure they developed norms. This was a mistake. Teams functioned just fine without norms until there was a conflict between team members or a team member decided not to follow through and participate fully. In other words, we didn't need norms until we did. We had counted on team members having good intentions and a willingness to participate in a PLC as professionals. We had not counted on the fact that the definitions of *good intentions* and *professionalism* are not a shared understanding. We learned that without an explicit and intentional set of norms and team members' full commitment, many of our teams struggled to collaborate.

We retraced our steps and retrained our teams on the importance of norms and strategies to develop and enforce them. We quickly learned that creating shared norms helped our teams collaborate at higher levels, and we eliminated many problems we had with team members not meeting their obligations. The eighteen critical issues provided our guiding coalition with a checklist that helped us comprehensively approach PLC development districtwide.

Understanding Common Structural Components and Implementation Models

The relationship between the critical structural components for PLC implementation must always be visible to all throughout the district. Before diving into implementation, all members of the organization—not just the guiding coalition—must be able to name the structural components, just like the vocabulary, and have a working knowledge of their purposes and functions. This common knowledge provides clear evidence of the district's commitment to long-term implementation and its willingness to support its schools, collaborative teams, and individual teachers. Figure 1.3 (page 24) illustrates the relationships between PLC implementation structural components.

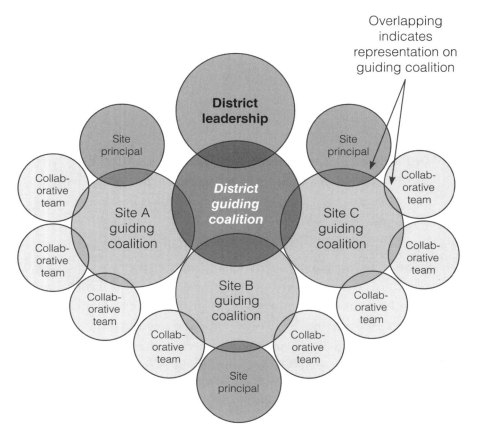

Figure 1.3: Relationship between implementation structures and positions.

District guiding coalitions can promote transparency and common knowledge across the district by posting their agendas and minutes, and individual schools' guiding coalitions can do the same.

Additionally, it's important for leaders to be familiar with the range of implementation plans commonly found in schools and districts in order to recognize their own model and whether it needs to be updated. In many cases, the implementation plan takes on an informal, non-specific, general quality. In these districts, when asked to describe their implementation plan, leaders will respond with generalizations and have difficulty detailing their goals or their conceptual picture of implementation. This is in comparison to districts that share a common language, have a road map, and establish clear goals and an explicit, step-by-step, formal implementation plan. Districts with formal plans often detail the work they need to do and the designated actions they will take through checklists and action plans. The following models illustrate the differences in implementation plans.

The Laissez-Faire Implementation Model

Laissez-faire, by definition, describes a system that forgoes the district office's interference during implementation beyond stating, "We are going to implement professional learning communities districtwide." Figure 1.4 portrays a school district that has defined its current reality. The superintendent has stated that to improve its current reality, the district will be implementing professional learning communities without defining a vision. This lack of vision or direction leaves all schools and teams guessing what is important and what their focus should be. In figure 1.4, the arrows emanating from the current reality represent random implementation acts the schools take as they work to "do" professional learning communities. Schools have complete autonomy to implement as they choose.

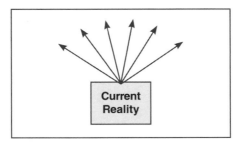

Figure 1.4: Laissez-faire implementation model.

Districts that have adopted this model, either intentionally or through acquiescence, tend to unevenly implement a districtwide PLC, as the biggest determining factor for success is the strength of site leadership. District leaders tend to consider the laissez-faire implementation model effective if schools that adopt it have success, but if success eludes those who adopt this model, district leaders have no solutions for them to improve.

The Bureaucratic Implementation Model

In the bureaucratic implementation model, or one-size-fits-all approach, the superintendent clearly states the district's commitment to moving to a PLC culture. The district clearly defines the current reality for all schools and provides an explicit and well-defined goal that exactly matches the superintendent's specifications. Additionally, the district defines the path to reach this goal with the expectation that each school shall follow this plan. The expectations and parameters are tight and leave no room for deviation. Schools are warned that deviation will not be accepted under any circumstances. The district makes no allowances for school decision making, tailoring for training, or implementation. Figure 1.5 illustrates this model.

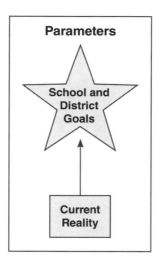

Figure 1.5: Bureaucratic implementation model.

In these districts, schools take on implementation as a matter of compliance with little or no buy-in. In this system, schools find growth in their technical capabilities as they understand the work's step-by-step process. Studying districts and schools that adopt this model, Joan Talbert (2010) notes, "They tend not to engage the cultural and political challenges of system change, nor to see change in developmental terms" (p. 561).

The Loose-Tight Implementation Model

The loose-tight implementation model combines the best elements of the bureaucratic implementation model with the autonomy of the laissez-faire implementation model. In this implementation model, the superintendent clearly states the district's commitment to forming a PLC culture. The district guiding coalition has worked with district leaders to define the PLC implementation vision and break it into clear expectations and parameters. It has provided clear school and district goals and shared the implementation training and foundational knowledge with the principals and site guiding coalitions. Knowing the goals and parameters, school teams are left to design their pathway to reach the established goals from their current reality. Principals and guiding coalitions at each school have the autonomy to design and implement their pathway through their collaboration. The district's role shifts to one of support as school teams strive to reach their established goals while working within implementation parameters. Figure 1.6 illustrates this model.

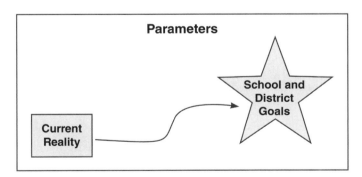

Figure 1.6: Loose-tight implementation model.

In the loose-tight implementation model, *tight* refers to the firmly set goal, parameters, or expectations. *Loose* refers to the school's site-specific implementation design. The site's principal and teams have ownership to collaborate, make modifications, work to overcome obstacles within their parameters, and focus on their goal. Technical as well as cultural elements come into play as teams work to implement their plans.

Richard DuFour and Robert Marzano (2011) see the need for a loose-tight approach, writing, "In effective districts, educators in individual schools enjoy some latitude within specified parameters, and the unique context of an individual school is recognized" (p. 30). As noted in *District Leadership That Works*, the district leadership establishes the "common work of schools within the district" that serves as "the glue holding the district together" (Marzano & Waters, 2009, p. 90).

The most effective implementation model—the loose-tight implementation model—provides clear, explicit expectations for the PLC model (the *tight*), while allowing schools the opportunity to make autonomous decisions for the site (the *loose*). The combination of a common vision and the loose-tight implementation guides the efforts of all staff as they move toward building collaborative teams across the district. Explicitly and intentionally developing a common district vision of PLCs provides a target for implementation, which allows for the work across the district to move in a focused and aligned manner.

Final Thoughts

To build a shared vision, the critical components for PLC implementation—and the goals, structures, and operations—must be visible to all throughout the district. These components form the foundation for the work. The model district leaders choose to turn the vision into reality has a direct impact on schools' buy-in and ownership. Principals and teachers will strive to implement at deeper and more successful levels when they see implementation not as a matter of compliance but one of ownership of their school's program. The loose-tight implementation model provides them the opportunity for ownership while retaining the district's shared vision.

Chapter 2

Empowering Site Leadership Through Staff Development and Training

District leadership has made it unequivocally clear to all those concerned that the district is developing a collaborative PLC culture. The guiding coalition has provided input on tailoring the message and fundamental rationale for moving to a collaborative culture. This is a critical stage for setting a firm foundation on which to implement PLCs districtwide. The efforts of district leaders and the work of the guiding coalition must lead to districtwide PLC rollout across school sites. This begins with the leaders of those sites: the principals.

Districts with high levels of initial implementation success first ensure that principals have a firm understanding of the fundamental foundations of professional learning communities. They equip principals with a working knowledge of PLC vocabulary and a road map of what teams are expected to do. District leaders cannot expect principals to teach, coach, and support others by simply handing them copies of *Learning by Doing* (DuFour et al., 2010). Principals will be responsible for their sites' PLC implementation, so district leaders must support them with specific principal training.

The plan for a districtwide PLC training program must be well thought out to ensure the understanding of PLC implementation grows in a systematic way. A single workshop or general training session provides an introduction but does little to support or sustain implementation. A well-thought-out plan ensures that time, energy, and money are not wasted, and it leads to sustained implementation and growth through the development of a common language.

Before designing a staff development plan, a district guiding coalition and principals must consider the question, "What stages of team development will we want to see?" To this end, I worked to design descriptors of the stages that teams move through as they deepen their learning and implementation. As teams implement they move through a series of five learning and implementation stages.

1. Learning stage

2. Literal stage

3. Refinement stage

4. Internalized stage

5. Innovative stage

Table 2.1 describes each stage in detail.

The spectrum of team learning frames the design of staff development by forcing planners to consider what necessary learning, training, and support can move their team or school from one level of PLC implementation to the next.

The most successful principal PLC training processes begin with a meeting with the superintendent. The superintendent specifically frames the rationale for PLCs and ensures that all principals

Table 2.1: The Spectrum of Team Learning

Learning Stage	Teams are learning the basic concepts, vocabulary, and processes of professional learning communities.
Literal Stage	Staff have developed a basic understanding of the PLC vocabulary and processes. The team can move through the process of a collaborative team through the use of notes and a flowchart.
Refinement Stage	The team understands PLC processes and is working to streamline its process and become more proficient in its practices.
Internalized Stage	The team fully grasps the processes and concepts of a PLC. The team's practices become an internalized part of what it does as a team.
Innovative Stage	The team now can use the PLC concepts and processes to problem solve, teach others in the organization, and apply team members' understanding to new situations.

understand the district leadership's level of commitment to full district implementation. Principals must clearly understand the district leadership's expectations of each principal's role in implementation. Without this intentional and explicit meeting, many principals will assume that PLC implementation is just another initiative and take a *wait-and-see* stance toward implementation. If not confronted with a firm commitment from the superintendent, the naysayer and wait-and-see principals will not move their schools forward. In a worst-case scenario, these principals may fuel pushback from naysayer teachers at their schools through negative statements or, worse, deliberate political gamesmanship. Principals should face no confusion as to the district's direction and commitment.

It is highly recommended that principals be trained together or, if the district is very large, in cohorts. To create collaborative districts, district leaders must provide principals with training opportunities that allow them to collaborate, learn together, and find best practices. In this way, principals have the opportunity to discuss and find meaning in the new PLC concepts presented to them. As practitioners, principals need time to collaborate to clearly see how implementation might look in their schools. They need to bounce ideas off one another and hear what others are planning.

The most successful training processes allow for team time throughout the training and at the end of each day. Team time allows the attendees to discuss what they have learned, share insights, raise questions, and build relevance. These discussions often lead to insights, best practices, and recommendations that are instrumental in refining workshops and trainings.

After the superintendent has unequivocally stated the district's direction and that principals will play a key role, he or she must propose a plan to principals that details trainings and expectations for implementation. Principals must support implementation at their site and possibly across the district by providing their instructional expertise, coaching, and attending training sessions with their staff.

Being Present for Principal Training

District leadership, please heed this cautionary and best-practices note: attend training with principals. Having the superintendent or a key district leader in attendance sends a clear message of commitment to principals. It provides district leaders with an opportunity to ensure that they send no mixed messages about the initiative's importance. In attending, district leaders can directly answer questions, reassure principals of the district's support, and act as a *dipstick* to measure buy-in and site leadership commitment. In the same way a mechanic first checks the dipstick to ensure that the necessary oil to run a car engine is present before turning the car key, leaders must first check to ensure that buy-in and commitment are present before training.

For example, consider the following. District X's superintendent voiced repeatedly the intention to implement PLCs across the district. The district formed a guiding coalition, planned training, selected a tremendous presenter, and began implementation with a principal workshop in August. Unfortunately, no district leaders attended because their "schedules would not allow it." The predominant comment on the workshop evaluations was "If this is important, then shouldn't the district superintendent be present? This time of year, I am busy too. Great workshop, but if the district leadership doesn't care, then this is dead on arrival."

District leaders must match principals' commitment by being present and engaged in order for district implementation to succeed.

Choosing a Presenter or Trainer

A strong first training for principals is one done by a practitioner who has documented success with PLCs at their schools. Hearing from a practitioner with proven success provides PLC implementation with credibility and relevance for principals. A presenter or trainer with a solid background can provide a clear, pragmatic path to school PLC implementation; address concerns; identify critical best practices for success; and point out potential pitfalls to avoid.

In 2004, I facilitated twenty-four principals who went to a two-day workshop with Richard and Rebecca DuFour, great presenters but also two highly successful principals and pioneers of the PLC at Work™ process with documented success in PLC implementation. Several principals in this group firmly believed that efforts to implement PLCs were just another of the latest educational fads. However, at the afternoon follow-up meeting, it became clear that these principals' stances had shifted significantly due to Rick and Becky's clear and pragmatic presentation. By the end of the workshop's second day, all twenty-four principals understood the district's direction and were willing to move forward with meaningful implementation. As one principal put it, "It is hard to argue with the common sense of how professional learning communities work to ensure learning." It became obvious that the turning point was the clear connection between concepts and pragmatic implementation. Principals were able to grasp the relevance of how PLCs could help them change their schools' culture and focus.

As previously noted, most principals have to-do lists they must accomplish on any given day. These lists are usually made up of urgent, important, and necessary items. As with all educators, principals' most valuable resources are time and energy. Therefore, training programs must help them see that implementation should be based on researched-based concepts, the necessity of key programmatic elements, and doable implementation. Schools must choose presenters based on their ability to ensure that training contains these critical elements.

First and foremost, those charged with locating and hiring a presenter or trainer must have a basic knowledge of PLCs. Choosing a presenter or trainer gives guiding coalition members and district leadership an outstanding opportunity, as they have already built a foundational understanding that will help them serve as a workshop selection committee. A workshop selection committee made up of guiding coalition members and district leaders can work to ensure that presenters are a solid match for trainees. The workshop selection committee should have the opportunity to speak with the presenter, discuss the presenter's background, provide a clear picture of the district's current implementation status, and supply the district's vision and plan.

Major pitfalls on the journey to district implementation include mismatching a presenter with an audience and selecting a presenter who does not understand the district's direction. For example, consider the following examples. District X hired a presenter for its principals without more than a brief phone conversation confirming dates and times. Presenter X arrived at the training and informed the principals in attendance that he had never been a principal. The audience disengaged within the first fifteen minutes of the workshop. The principals did not see the presenter as a practitioner, so the presenter immediately lacked credibility with the principals. Also, consider District Z, who hired Presenter Z without discussing the district's vision or implementation plan. Throughout the workshop, Presenter Z laid out her implementation plan, which differed significantly from the district's plan. The principals' confusion was palpable. Evaluations of the workshop bore out the principals' confusion and frustration: "What are we doing? I am hearing two separate stories of what we are going to do. Can we please get on the same page?" The workshop caused principals to doubt the doability of implementation, and confusion led to a major setback in the district's rollout.

Selection committees should never choose presenters for any presentation, workshop, or training without explicit and intentional selection. In selecting a presenter, keep the following basic questions in mind.

- Is this person an expert with a proven history of successful implementation?

- Will my team relate to this expert's background and accomplishments?

- Does this expert understand our expectations for training and how this training fits into our overall district plan?

Training Teachers

District leaders must also clearly think out and plan the jump from training principals to training site staff to ensure that teachers fully comprehend the rationale and benefits for becoming a PLC district. Those charged with presenting the rationale and implementation plan to teachers must have a firm grasp on and carry the same message to all teachers across the district. The guiding coalition, district leadership, and principals can play major roles in explaining the district's rationale and plan for PLC implementation. Teachers will need a frame of reference as implementation unfolds across the district, so they will not feel surprised or confused when hearing about training or district efforts to support implementation.

Two major considerations in planning for teacher training are the number of teachers in the district and funding. Schools must balance how many teachers can be trained at a time, consider workshop costs, and determine the availability of substitute teachers and training locations in designing this next step.

Training Site Guiding Coalitions

With the principals trained, the focus must shift to forming a guiding coalition at each school site and building its fundamental understanding of professional learning communities. Selecting site guiding coalition members resembles district guiding coalition methods but with fewer staff to choose from. Careful selection is recommended. As with district guiding coalitions, school guiding coalitions must include members with influence and credibility and who represent all grade levels and departments at the site. Selection should not be taken lightly; the guiding coalition must be made up of those who will ensure successful implementation at the site.

In some instances, principals may take recommendations from grade levels and departments; they may ask for volunteers or even select members based on seniority. All are flawed methods for building a guiding coalition. These methods may result in a guiding coalition that provides a skewed perspective of implementation success tainted by personal agendas, or worse yet—a lack of interest in successful implementation. As Robert Eaker often says, "Some principals put more effort into building a successful football coaching staff than they do a productive guiding coalition."

Focusing on influence, credibility, and representation in member selection ensures that the guiding coalition provides critical feedback. It supports an open flow of communication to tailor and resolve site implementation issues. School guiding coalitions provide clear perspectives from differing vantage points than the district, which helps members understand site issues and seek solutions that will propel teams toward deeper, more meaningful collaboration.

As with the district guiding coalition, the site guiding coalition needs to welcome members and explain the coalition's purpose. Members must have a clear understanding of their roles and how they are crucial to the guiding coalition's success and the school's role in districtwide PLC implementation. Understanding each member's importance and honoring his or her willingness to participate are foundational to the entire guiding coalition's belief that collaborative work will lead to positive changes in culture, practice, and student achievement.

Following the district guiding coalition's lead, school guiding coalitions must build their knowledge of the fundamentals of PLCs. School guiding coalitions should go through the same training as the principals and district leaders with the same trainer, if possible. The uniformity of presentations allows all trainees to share a common PLC vocabulary and vision. Using the same presenter ensures that all who have been through training are guaranteed the same foundation from which to build at their sites.

The site guiding coalition, if possible, should receive training as a team so that all members are together, including the principal. Having the members together, as with the principals' training, allows them to have discussions, seek relevance, and plan for implementation. The principal's attendance and active engagement in the workshop signal a level of commitment to the guiding coalition. The principal, who has already been trained, can assist the team in developing a clearer understanding of how implementation will look at the school site.

As with the principal workshop, the presenter should provide time for teams to discuss potential implementation issues. At the end of each workshop day, teams should meet in team time to develop their implementation plan based on the foundational elements they learned that day. The presenter should also be available to answer team questions during this time. During this workshop, the guiding coalition, with the principal's support, should complete a clearly written and sequenced implementation plan for its school site. All guiding coalition members should not only know the rationale behind PLCs but also have the ability to provide basic foundational training, support, and explanations to colleagues at their site.

Choosing a Kickoff Path

There are several common paths that districts may take to accelerate the implementation of professional learning communities districtwide. Following are three paths to consider.

The General Session Presentation

Often, districts will kick off PLC implementation with a keynote speaker at a general session event at the beginning of the academic year. This type of approach can be very effective in developing enthusiasm, but it runs the risk of being more of an event than a meaningful foundation builder. In many districts, the general session kickoff is an annual event. Teachers in these districts have come to expect a witty presentation but generally leave with the attitude that "this too shall pass."

The general session presentation can be effective if the district has already prepared guiding coalitions to build on the basic knowledge and enthusiasm produced at a general session. The guiding coalition members can help fill in the general session presentation's gaps and unanswered questions. They can channel the presentation's enthusiasm back into the PLC implementation plan they designed.

The School-by-School Workshop

Many districts train one school staff at a time throughout the academic year. This plan can leave a district fragmented with no way to adequately support its schools. Without forming and using input from a school guiding coalition with foundational knowledge, this training runs the risk of assuming a one-size-fits-all approach. In most cases of a one-size-fits-all approach, leadership has usually done little to solicit input to tailor training to align with the district's vision or the staff's buy-in or prior knowledge and experiences. Oftentimes, the training design is a canned professional development program that lacks any tailoring to the district's vision or needs. Principals without a site guiding coalition's input to guide and design implementation must try to build buy-in and support on their own during a staffwide workshop. Without the guiding coalition's guidance, principals are often confronted with naysayers who seek to stall or kill the PLC initiative by seeking to punch holes in the rationale throughout the workshop. The outcome of the school-by-school workshop plan depends on the presenter's quality and competence as he or she works to build support for the principal and initiative during the workshop.

School-by-school training is also problematic because some schools receive training late in the school year when their schools' patterns and schedules have already been established. Making changes in teacher behavior patterns becomes very difficult as the year progresses. These schools tend to acknowledge the training but then put off implementation until the following academic year because they already have a plan for the current academic year.

Optional Training

Optional training allows schools to choose when, and if, to send teachers for training. Training depends on the principal's decision regarding when, and if, teachers will participate. The optional plan is rarely, if ever, successful in implementing PLCs across a district.

The *optional* label sends a message to principals that district leadership's commitment to PLC implementation is, at best, lukewarm. The optional component says to principals that this plan may or may not be around next year. The district that pursues this implementation path wastes time and money. Teachers who do attend will feel unsupported, and those who do not choose to participate will never move beyond the status quo. Optional training is nothing more than lip service.

The Ideal Approach

District and site guiding coalitions create a cadre of trained leaders who can help lead and facilitate site-level PLC implementation because of their shared knowledge, vocabulary, and vision. The trained leaders set the stage to learn while doing the implementation work at the school site. If the district chooses not to do a general session presentation, the site guiding coalition and principal must ensure that the entire staff know the rationale and vocabulary they will need for PLC implementation. Staff should receive a vision of how implementation will look at their school. The principal and guiding coalition need to work together closely to plan for introductory and subsequent training sessions to further basic learning and support implementation. Using the workshop agenda and materials from the district-provided site guiding coalition training, the site guiding coalition tailors the site's plan.

I highly recommend that the site guiding coalition work closely with the principal to schedule their plan. Coalition members should keep in mind that most school districts have academic calendars with the following parameters.

- One to two weeks of preservice summer training
- Thirty-six weeks per school year
- Eighteen weeks per semester
- Twelve weeks per trimester

- Nine weeks per quarter

- Roughly 180 school days

Using these parameters, guiding coalitions should consider setting implementation goals and expectations. Schools that have proven to be the most successful in PLC implementation establish key expectations for training and foundational work as their teams move from learning the process to implementing and refining it. Schools whose guiding coalitions have developed a plan can focus on the work and measure their progress, diagnose areas of concern, and seek appropriate solutions and supports from their district. These schools have made implementation explicit, intentional, and doable, such as in the sample plan featured in figure 2.1.

Travis Braxton Elementary Professional Learning Community Implementation Plan

Summer Week: Districtwide Professional Learning Community Training

- The site guiding coalition goes through two days of district-provided PLC training.

- The guiding coalition and Principal Tracy meet and develop an implementation plan for the school year based on training.

- The guiding coalition plans members' roles in training and implementation.

Preservice Week: One Day of Whole-Staff Training Prior to the Start of the School Year

- Principal Tracy introduces the PLC rationale and vision to the staff.

- Guiding coalition members introduce and train staff on key components of PLCs.

  - Team commitments and norms

  - The four questions of a PLC

  - The district road map for PLC work

  - Essential standards, common formative assessments, and the use of data

  - Reteaching and enrichment

  - The guiding coalition's implementation plan for the year

Figure 2.1: Sample school implementation plan.   Continued →

School Year: Weeks 1–2

- Teams frame commitments and norms.
- Teams review summative data (state testing results) of incoming students.
- Teams set essential standards or skills and pacing for the year.
- Teams prepare to work on their first essential standard or skill.

School Year: Weeks 3–6

- All teams have completed the entire PLC road map of activities for their first essential standard or skill. Each guiding coalition member reports his or her team's progress toward implementing the PLC process through data review, instructional best practices, reteaching, and enrichment.

School Year: Weeks 7–10

- All teams move to their second essential standard or skill and implement the district road map.
- Teams that believe they have reached the refinement level may modify their pacing of essential standards or skills based on what they have learned of the PLC process and road map.

School Year: Weeks 11–17

- Teams continue to move through their essential standards or skills following the PLC road map.
- Guiding coalition members report their teams' essential standard or skill results, provide evidence of team learning growth on the spectrum of team learning, and seek support when needed at weekly guiding coalition meetings.

School Year: Week 18—First Semester Review of Growth and Recommendations for the Second Semester

- The guiding coalition leads a general staff meeting to review first-semester growth and recommendations using a plus/delta chart.
- Teams review and provide evidence of their placement on the spectrum of team learning.
- The guiding coalition leads discussion and charts areas that need greater support and learning, which should take place during the second semester.

School Year: Week 19—First Week of the Second Semester

- Teams review summative test data from the first semester and discuss reteaching needs.
- Teams review their pacing guides of essential standards or skills.

School Year: Weeks 20–28

- Teams continue to move through their essential standards or skills following the PLC road map.
- Guiding coalition members report their teams' essential standard or skill results, provide evidence of team learning growth on the spectrum of team learning, and seek support when needed at weekly guiding coalition meetings.

School Year: Weeks 29–34—State Testing Window

- Teams adjust to ensure that critical essential standards or skills are reinforced.
- Teams closely coordinate their testing dates to support one another.
- Teams use the PLC road map on a quick cycle to ensure mastery of essential standards or skills.

School Year: Week 35—Second Semester Review of Growth and Recommendations for the Next Semester

- The guiding coalition leads a general staff meeting to review second-semester growth and recommendations using a plus/delta chart.
- Teams review and provide evidence of their placement on the spectrum of team learning.
- The guiding coalition leads discussion and charts areas that need greater support and learning, which should take place during the summer or prior to the next academic year.

School Year: Week 36—Final Week of School

- Teams review their pacing of essential standards or skills and discuss how they might improve their PLC work for the next academic year.
- Teams discuss additional training and support that are needed.
- Teams finalize their placement on the spectrum of team learning by providing evidence of their growth.

Summer Week: Guiding Coalition Only

- The guiding coalition meets after school is out to review the growth and progress of its PLC implementation.
- The guiding coalition formalizes plans for improving and supporting implementation for the next academic year.
- The guiding coalition finalizes a presentation regarding its PLC implementation efforts that will be available to all school sites across the district for training and reference purposes.

Final Thoughts

Schools that are not explicit and intentional in their planning tend to make uneven progress with some teams moving quickly while other teams flounder or push back with little or no buy-in.

At a school with no plan, it is not uncommon to find individual teams that are successfully implementing the district's PLC vision. These successful teams usually have a strong teacher leader who has bought in, sees the value of PLCs for teachers and students, and is willing to lead. This leader can explain the rationale, facilitate training, and explain the school's vision for implementing PLCs so that team members understand. These teams tend to be self-reliant and find ways to overcome in spite of their school's poor implementation plans.

Teams that flounder or push back against PLCs have little buy-in because they have no sequential plan of development and growth to reference or guide them. Naysayers on these teams see no plan and have no foundational knowledge or vision. They cite poor school implementation as a sign of a lack of commitment for PLCs. Without a functioning plan for the site guiding coalition to reference, these schools waste time and energy as other schools in the district with plans begin to move through the stages of learning and implementation.

Schools with knowledgeable and engaged principals who support and facilitate the efforts of each site's guiding coalition to develop a doable implementation plan allow their teams to overcome obstacles, grow in their effective knowledge, and internalize implementation. These schools' guiding coalitions gain a deeper sense of buy-in and ownership for their PLC development, which allows them to hold themselves accountable for their teams' development and results. Reciprocal accountability thus becomes a reality in these schools.

Chapter 3

Monitoring to Sustain Momentum

We've all heard the phrase "What gets monitored gets done." This admonishment seems to indicate that if we simply monitor district-wide PLC implementation, then it will happen. What gets monitored may get done, but are you measuring what really matters? The frightening part is that we have the potential to monitor the wrong things. Monitoring the wrong things can lead to an enormous waste of time and energy and turn collaboration into a bureaucratic paper chase.

On the other hand, we cannot forgo monitoring and assume that all schools and teams are implementing the PLC process as planned. Following the "No news is good news" strategy tends to lead to a district administrative mirage of successful implementation that may or may not be actually happening at the sites. This type of monitoring strategy provides no feedback to tailor or modify training and support. In this case, we are hoping for the best, but if district leadership is to effectively provide support, coaching, and guidance as schools move toward internalization, monitoring must take place.

Joan Talbert (2010) contrasts two approaches to monitoring:

> A "bureaucratic strategy" uses traditional management tools of directives and rules, prescribed routines, and sanctions for compliance as ways to promote change. A "professional strategy" uses tools of decision-making structures, professional expertise and knowledge resources, and leader modeling and feedback to engender change. (p. 561)

As monitoring is critical for successful PLC implementation, school leaders must ensure monitoring actually promotes deep, sustained implementation. Additionally, school staff must see monitoring as support, not a compliance evaluation of their efforts.

Measuring the Right Things

When something unimportant is measured, it tends to result in resentment and pushback from those who do the important work. Monitor the wrong things, and you will likely get the wrong behaviors. Ensuring districtwide implementation and improving performance, in most cases, mean changing the focus and behaviors of those who are implementing by providing feedback and opportunities for learning. Monitoring should be seen as coaching, not inspection.

The first step in monitoring effectively is to determine the priorities that schools and teams should focus on. According to Joseph Juran, "Without a standard, there is no logical basis for making a decision or taking action" (as cited in Williamson, 2006). We need to compare a school's or district's current reality to established goals and "take intelligent, consistent actions . . . to eliminate problems" in our efforts to achieve our goals (Williamson, 2006). Monitoring focused only on programmatic elements tends to narrow school's focus to short-term criteria for success. Monitoring only school culture issues diverts focus from "grappling with both bigger and more fine-grained issues of student learning and teaching that ground effective PLC interventions and create shared accountability for results" (Talbert, 2010). While districts that focus wholly on numerical data tend to get mired in their schools' and teams' inspection and compliance, using monitoring as a tool for coaching and continuous improvement can establish collective responsibility, best practices, and a positive change in culture and focus.

Furthermore, if we are to ensure effective districtwide implementation, then it makes little sense to centralize monitoring to just district leadership. To provide timely feedback and coaching, monitoring should function at all levels of implementation: team, site guiding coalition, district guiding coalition, and district leadership.

Consider the following example. District Q moves to implement PLCs at every school in its district. District leaders train their principals and site guiding coalitions and send them back to their schools with instructions to train and implement teacher teams. After the training, the principal informs the teacher teams that they will meet a number of times and regularly submit their agendas, minutes, common formative assessments, and assessment results to the principal and site guiding coalition to monitor their progress. This could be a recipe for success or failure depending on what happens next.

Not much will change if the principal and site guiding coalition put the collected artifacts into storage, return a vague message of "Nice job," or give feedback a week later, if at all. The benefits and value of collaboration will not take root in this systemic format. Another compliance is checked off and then forgotten.

Instead, if the principal and site guiding coalition team monitor, review key artifacts and provide timely written or verbal feedback, meet regularly with teams to share successes, assist with frustrations, and suggest next steps, the focus has a greater chance of success. When leaders step in to provide site guiding coalitions with time and direction for shared learning and collaboration, schools see the importance of monitoring. The district expectation is that staff implement PLCs with the support of the site guiding coalition and principal through reflective monitoring, leading to a focus on growth and development of the team process and individual team members. Table 3.1 (page 48) provides a monitoring protocol.

Table 3.1: Monitoring Protocol

Monitoring Group	Group Being Monitored	Qualities Being Monitored
Grade-level and department teams	Team members	• Common formative assessment data correlated with instructional practices • Reteaching and enrichment data focused on best practices • Achievement of SMART goals
Site guiding coalition	Grade-level and departmental teams	• Numerical data showing student achievement and learning from common formative assessments and focusing on summative data and achievement of SMART goals • Programmatic artifacts—norms, agendas, minutes, rubric ratings, and the achievement of SMART goals • Cultural artifacts—self-assessment surveys, attendance records, deviations from norms, and specific interpersonal conflicts
District leadership and district guiding coalition	Site guiding coalition	• Numerical data showing student achievement and learning by grade level and department and focusing on summative data and achievement of SMART goals • Programmatic artifacts demonstrating the range of team progress—norms, agendas, minutes, rubric ratings, and the achievement of SMART goals • Cultural artifacts—overall school self-assessment surveys, team participation and buy-in information, and staff's programmatic concerns

Numerical Data

Focusing on student learning data must be the major focus of site-based PLC implementation. The achievement and learning data generated from common formative assessments of standards and skills provide feedback on what students have learned, who needs enrichment, and what needs reteaching. These learning data must also inform the team and its members of the effectiveness of the instructional strategies. Teams must be able to connect common formative assessment data to best practices. Team members become interdependent through the discussions they have and the correlations they make regarding the data and their instructional practices. The numerical data generated as teams work are valuable evidence of a team's effectiveness. This can also be said about the summative data that teams review as they work. State testing, end-of-unit exams, and semester final results all provide valuable evidence of student learning and team effectiveness.

Monitoring SMART (strategic and specific, measurable, attainable, results oriented, time bound; Conzemius & O'Neill, 2014) goals can also function as a tool for assessing team and school progress, but this comes with a cautionary note. Whether a team meets or does not meet its SMART goals may depend more on the team's level of mastery or proficiency than its success with instructional practices. For example, all of School A's teams have regularly met their SMART goals because they established low thresholds and expectations for student learning. In School B, all teams reported that they rarely met their SMART goals because they set their expected student passage rate at 100 percent—an admirable goal but less than realistic. Monitoring SMART goals requires that the ability for the team or school to meet the goal is actually realistic. Simply meeting or not meeting SMART goals does not go far enough to prove successful team implementation of the PLC process.

Programmatic Artifacts

As stated in chapter 1 (pages 20–22), school sites and districts should have eighteen critical issues in place to carry out PLC implementation across all sites. The eighteen critical issues are not merely a checklist. Affirming the presence of each critical issue does not represent quality implementation. To effectively monitor and provide meaningful feedback to teams and schools, districts should consider using rubrics.

Districts can use two types of rubrics for programmatic monitoring. First, the district guiding coalition can draw from research-based rubrics that contain critical elements with extensive and clear exemplars. For example, leaders could use some of the excellent rubrics from *Learning by Doing* (DuFour et al., 2010). (Visit **go.solution-tree.com/PLCbooks** for sample rubrics.) Second, the district guiding coalition can develop a rubric based on the spectrum of team learning stages (page 30) and tailor the language and focus of PLC implementation that the district has designed. Developing a district rubric allows the district guiding coalition to control the rubric's complexity, number of elements to consider, and range of exemplars. In my experience, the more complex the rubric, the harder it becomes to calibrate users' understanding of the elements and exemplars. This difficulty leads to misunderstandings and, eventually, a resistance to use the rubric. Thus, Sanger Unified School District developed a simple rubric to begin the implementation process at its school sites. (See figure 3.1.) (Although I've included the innovation stage in this sample rubric, I've moved away from defining the innovative stage in detail when working with schools. The key to the innovative stage is taking the internalized stage and building on it in ways that are yet to be defined—thus innovative. With the innovative stage, teams take the specific lessons they've learned in implementation and think of new ways to promote learning while retaining the critical concepts of collaboration.)

Foundational PLC Elements	Learning Stage	Literal Stage	Refinement Stage	Internalized Stage	Innovative Stage
Establishing a Collaborative Culture Educators work together in collaborative teams to achieve student learning.	Teams meet regularly (weekly, biweekly, or monthly) during the school year.	Collaborative teams develop written norms and establish learning goals that clarify expectations and commitments.	Teams focus on prearranged topics that impact student learning, and they make revisions to goals to improve team effectiveness.	Teams honor their collective commitments to each other and their students in order to maximize learning.	Teams garner buy-in to collective commitments from parents, support staff, and others with an impact on student learning.
Having a Guaranteed Curriculum Educators establish what they want their students to learn.	Educators use district-developed curriculum guide resources.	Educators work together to define essential learning and establish pacing.	Educators build shared knowledge of current content standards, unpack high-stakes assessments to clarify essential learning, and adjust instruction based on formative assessments.	Educators continually refine essential learning and guarantee a viable instructional program for all students.	Educators develop a guaranteed curriculum that incorporates the efforts of grade levels below and above theirs or courses above and below their content areas.

Figure 3.1: Sample rubric based on the spectrum of team learning.

Continued ↓

Foundational PLC Elements	Learning Stage	Literal Stage	Refinement Stage	Internalized Stage	Innovative Stage
Using Common Assessments Educators determine if all students have learned what educators want them to learn through the use of formative and summative assessments.	Educators use benchmark assessments several times throughout the year.	Educators analyze student work and assessments and discuss common criteria.	Educators consistently apply common criteria to assess student work and discuss formative instructional practices.	Educators consistently utilize formative instructional practices, including common assessments, to gather evidence of student learning.	Educators use data to determine best instructional practices to ensure learning for all students. Educators continuously improve instructional practices based on learning data.
Ensuring Learning Educators respond when some students have not learned what is considered essential learning.	Educators use school or district classes, established specialized pull-out or after-school programs, and curriculum resources when students are identified for intervention.	Educators provide students with additional time and support that do not remove the students from new direct instruction when they experience difficulty.	Educators develop and utilize a timely, directive, and systemic plan for students when they experience difficulty.	Educators coordinate a flexible, supportive, and proactive intervention system for students who experience difficulty.	Educators implement a comprehensive, systematic, flexible, multitiered support system (response to intervention) to address learning needs requiring more intensive interventions.

Foundational PLC Elements	Learning Stage	Literal Stage	Refinement Stage	Internalized Stage	Innovative Stage
Enriching Learning Educators extend and enrich learning for students who have demonstrated mastery.	Educators use school or district classes, established enrichment pull-out or after-school programs, and curriculum resources when students are identified for enrichment.	Educators provide time and support for enrichment during the school day for those who have moved beyond essential learning.	Educators develop and utilize a timely, directive, and systemic plan for students who have moved beyond essential learning.	Educators coordinate a flexible, supportive, and proactive system for students who have moved beyond essential learning.	Educators implement a comprehensive and challenging program for students who consistently prove mastery of the essential learning.

Source: W. Richard Smith, Sanger Unifed School District, 2011.
Visit go.solution-tree.com/PLCbooks for a reproducible version of this figure.

As Sanger Unified learned, the power of using a rubric is that it can be tailored to point to critical implementation components while providing quality exemplars that can determine current team and school status and the next steps to take. Rubrics are not only a crucial tool for the status of a team or school in implementation but also a coaching document that identifies strengths and weaknesses. A rubric provides teams and schools with considerations for how they might deepen and refine their work. Teams should focus on three critical questions when they review their current status on a rubric.

1. What actions can we take as a team to move to the next level of quality exemplars on the rubric?

2. What outside support or training do we need to move to the next level of quality exemplars on the rubric?

3. When can we expect to meet the quality exemplars, and can we commit to this time line as a team or school?

A cautionary note on using rubrics for district leadership and site leadership: rubrics should not be seen as an evaluation of quality but as a means of targeting areas needing guidance and support. Utilizing a rubric as an evaluation tool quickly sends the message that monitoring is a bureaucratic exercise focused on accountability. Teams quickly deduce that compliance is more important than quality. A rubric should always be seen as a coaching tool to further the growth and development of implementation.

In conjunction with rubrics, those monitoring implementation (whether district guiding coalition, school guiding coalition, or school team) should also review school and team artifacts. These artifacts may include agendas, minutes, and common formative assessments. As stated previously, schools and teams should receive feedback regarding these documents. Those monitoring should strive to validate each team's and school's work as well as offer recommendations for improvement. They should not request artifacts that cannot be reviewed in a timely manner and with timely feedback. Therefore, those monitoring implementation must be thoughtful in what they request to ensure timeliness of review and feedback. Requesting reams of documents and not providing feedback lead to resentment and cynicism from teams and schools who will quickly perceive monitoring as an inspection. Choose wisely what you request, and work diligently to provide feedback.

Cultural Artifacts

Monitoring a team's and school's collaborative culture can be the most difficult. When I visit schools and districts, educators often tell me that a particular school or team has a *toxic* or *uncooperative* culture. The first question I ask is, "On what scale is this being judged?" Measuring culture can be as elusive as the definition of the word *culture*.

If we are to coach teams to deeper implementation, then we must have elements of culture to reference for improvement. Using Margaret Wheatley's (2006), Tim Dalmau (2000), and Steve Zuieback's (2012) work on developing a positive culture, monitoring focuses on four distinct elements.

1. **Information:** Does the team ensure the flow and sharing of critical information between team members?

2. **Relationships:** Do team members maintain professional relationships focused on their work on what is best for students instead of *buddy* relationships focused on adult agendas and needs?

3. **Identity:** Do team members see themselves as interdependent and mutually accountable parts of a team that is focused on a common goal?

4. **Trust:** Is trust exemplified by positive actions from all members in the areas of information, relationships, and identity?

Figure 3.2 illustrates these elements.

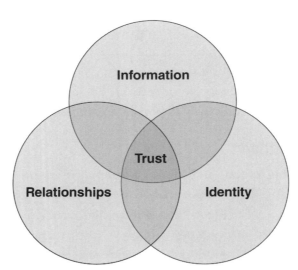

Figure 3.2: Positive culture.

The specific monitoring strategies and tools for reviewing these elements must provide critical information that results in feedback for teams and schools. Surveys and ratings are commonly used to determine the current status of a team's and school's culture. (Visit **go.solution-tree.com/PLCbooks** for reproducible sample surveys.) However, while survey and rating results often point out symptoms, they do not uncover causal issues for low ratings or survey remarks.

Interviews should always be the follow-up to any monitoring survey or rating activity. During interviews, team members provide critical background information that will allow monitors to understand the causes behind ratings or survey results. In interviewing a team, those monitoring should seek to gain insight and begin to formulate recommendations for discussion with the team. Often teams involved in interviews formulate their own solutions while discussing their ratings or survey results. Again, those monitoring must give feedback that is well thought out and specific to the cultural elements (see figure 3.2) that need improvement. Feedback can take the form of a written response or an additional meeting.

Those monitoring may also find that teams' meeting minutes may point out areas needing cultural improvement. In particular, minutes may indicate team members who are late or missing, conflicts that arise, or the inability to reach team consensus. Again, issues from the minutes should be categorized into the four cultural elements.

Final Thoughts

During districtwide PLC implementation, it is critical that district leaders and the district guiding coalition remember that teachers, teams, and schools have two critical resources that should not be squandered: time and energy. It is a high-stakes endeavor to monitor and implement systems for supporting the work of schools in such an intensely pressurized environment.

What I've noticed in successful schools *and* poorly performing schools is that what gets monitored—and supported—gets done. District leadership, the district guiding coalition, principals, and site guiding coalitions must focus on the most important elements that will support and move implementation forward. Ask too much, and resentment and cynicism will appear. Ask too little, and coaching and support will be unfocused. Effective monitoring sends the message, "This work is so important that we have taken the time to review it to support your growth and continued success."

Districts, schools, and teams that have successfully implemented the PLC process regularly share experiences and ideas with their colleagues and support them. School and district leaders and district and site guiding coalitions monitor teams, coach them, and facilitate feedback based on critical elements that will deepen districtwide implementation toward internalization.

Chapter 4

Ensuring Sustainability Through Ongoing Commitment and Implementation

Even after a successful year, many collaborative programs fail due to the lack of sustained effort. Maintaining commitment to change over time requires resolve, monitoring, and a steadfast focus on the benefits of collaboration (Mehaffey, 2001). District leaders must continue to embrace the vision, monitor progress, and clearly restate their support for districtwide PLC implementation. Proactive district leaders must have the skills to keep the soul of the PLC initiative alive and relevant to the needs of the district, schools, teams, and classroom teachers.

It cannot appear that district leaders shifted their attention and direction after one year of work. Anything less than continued, clearly stated commitment from district leadership will prove cynics correct and doom any future initiatives from district leadership to failure. It will also demoralize the work of those who bought into and supported PLC implementation efforts and make them think twice before buying into district plans. The stakes for the district's continued commitment are high and cannot be minimized.

The investment and efforts to build the guiding coalitions, provide training, and ensure adequate monitoring and coaching establish a firm district foundation for continued learning and implementation. Sustaining these efforts for multiple years moves implementation from learning and collaborating to "This is what our district does." After the second year of implementation at Sanger Unified, I was standing near a group of teachers at a conference, and one turned to a colleague from a neighboring district and declared, "We are a professional learning community district. We work together." The statement signaled to me that we at Sanger Unified had transformed districtwide PLC implementation from something we did to who we are and how we educate our students. Continued commitment to PLC implementation had moved teachers to understand that this is what we do, and it is not going away.

Celebrating Wins

It is critical for district leaders to validate each school's and team's work by recognizing the short-term wins of successful implementation. This recognition fuels achievement and continued growth. Schools must celebrate wins publicly but with the admonition that they are continuing the journey toward deeper implementation and learning for all students' benefit. As Marc Johnson often says in workshops, "There is no destination called *good enough*." Recognition is critical to validate teachers' and teams' efforts, but it should also serve to motivate and bring new energy to their efforts to internalize the PLC process so that they can ensure all students achieve.

In *Learning by Doing*, DuFour et al. (2010) identify declaring victory too soon as a common mistake in the change process. They write:

> Until change initiatives become anchored in the culture, they are fragile and subject to regression. Handled properly, the celebration of short-term wins can give the change initiative the credibility it needs to tackle bigger, more substantive problems. Handled improperly, this celebration can contribute to the complacency that is lethal to the change process. (p. 52)

District leaders can celebrate short-term wins in the following ways. They can take time at a staff meeting to publicly recognize a team for sharing best instructional practices teachers learned through collaboration. Also, recognizing a team's efforts in reteaching students who did not learn initially acknowledges and validates its work. Such acknowledgement and validation must be sincere and noteworthy and consistently given to teams that are making progress. We must be as willing and quick to recognize and celebrate growth and successes as we are to point out deficiencies or implementation issues. Positive public acknowledgement serves as a celebration that reinforces and renews the work of implementation as teams strive toward the district vision.

Refreshing Parameters and Expectations

The district guiding coalition in conjunction with district leadership must also review monitoring data to re-establish implementation goals and the parameters that schools must work within as they seek to deepen implementation. Goals must move the district and its schools and teams toward reaching the internalized stage of PLC implementation. District goals must be, as stated again, clear and explicit. District leaders must convey the goals to principals and site guiding coalitions so there are no misunderstandings as to the expectations.

Parameters, the *tight* part of the loose-tight implementation model (page 27), of what will be expected from schools and teams should accompany the goals. These parameters may or may not change from previous years, but district leaders must restate them clearly and explicitly to the sites. The district guiding coalition may need to review its monitoring rubrics to ensure the alignment of goals, parameters, and rubric exemplars.

The Golden Gate Staff Development Plan

The Golden Gate Bridge stands at the mouth of the San Francisco Bay. This massive structure is constantly under attack from the waves, salt air, and winds that flow through the mouth of the bay. To protect the bridge, workers continuously paint it. They paint the bridge fully, and when they finish, they paint the bridge again. Their work is never truly finished. Their protective paint ensures that the bridge will never deteriorate, rust, and crumble. With each subsequent coat of paint, the painters protect and enrich the bridge and ensure that it will stand for years to come.

Ongoing PLC training must take on this same strategy. Using information gained through monitoring, district leaders and the district guiding coalition must plan training that deepens, enriches, and supports PLC implementation. District leadership, the district guiding coalition, principals, and site guiding coalitions should be retrained with a focus on elements that monitoring pointed out as areas of need. This *repainting* should focus on deeper discussions about implementation, advanced facilitation, and problem solving. Training should only be as long as necessary to address these critical issues. It may not be necessary to spend multiple days in additional staff development to repaint.

In districts where retraining of previously trained site leadership has taken place, often, site leaders find mutual concerns or problems at multiple schools that were never discussed openly. These retraining sessions provide support for collaborative focus on deeper implementation. Often, several site guiding coalitions struggle to overcome an obstacle that another school in the same district had solved. The retraining sessions thus help expand best practices across the district as teams learn and share together.

Cohort Training

In an effort to deepen knowledge and expertise at school sites, districts should consider selecting a second cohort of teachers from each site to go through the initial PLC training. This training should match the training that principals, the district guiding coalition, and site guiding coalitions underwent previously. Allowing more teachers to participate adds another trained teacher to each team. Thus, with each subsequent cycle of training, teams should add additional cohorts.

Once again, it's critical that the principal attend trainings with subsequent cohorts. The principal's attendance signifies the importance of training teachers to embrace the school's goals of ensuring learning for all teachers and students. It can also be helpful for district leaders to attend, as with the earlier trainings, so that all attendees can see the district's commitment to PLC implementation.

Districts that utilize the cohort approach for continued training gain programmatic and cultural benefits. Teachers returning from subsequent cohort training bring new excitement, ideas, and perspectives to their teams. The new energy reignites and re-energizes teams' and schools' desires to collaborate with a deepened focus on student learning. The energy newly trained team members bring back often propels teams to the internalized stage (see page 30).

By training additional staff, schools deepen their pool of prospective site guiding coalition members. This also creates a deeper pool for selecting replacement or additional district guiding coalition members. Both site and district guiding coalitions will need to replace members as time continues. Some districts actually have a term limit for serving on both site and district guiding coalitions, which makes having a deeper pool essential.

Avoiding Complacency

District and site guiding coalitions must continue to provide monitoring, coaching, feedback, and targeted support. As years of successful implementation continue, there is a tendency for PLCs to become complacent in monitoring team and school implementation. This is a slippery path to losing the gains made through successful implementation.

For example, consider the following. District V's successful guiding coalition initially held monthly meetings as it strived to introduce and implement PLCs districtwide. As the district's success grew, the district guiding coalition reduced its meetings to once per semester. Its complacency and reduction in meetings led to a lack of monitoring. Without monitoring, the collaborative benefits the district gained began to deteriorate. As teachers retired, principals moved to different schools, and new teachers got hired, schools' dynamics and PLC functions also changed. Teams that were functioning at the internalized stage slid back to the literal stage (see page 30). Without consistent monitoring, time passed without giving teams the support they needed to arrest their losses. By the end of the third year of the slide, District V was no longer a true PLC.

Without monitoring progress, necessary adjustments, support, and coaching cannot be applied or directed. Continuous improvement is based on continuous monitoring, which works to ensure sustainability. Fullan (2010) alludes to this in his book *Motion Leadership*: "Put directly, communication during implementation is far more important than communication prior to implementation" (p. 26). The need to communicate status in relation to the implementation goals must continue and have prevalence for the district and its schools to sustain deep PLC implementation.

Final Thoughts

Districtwide PLC implementation that brings about collaboration focused on improving student achievement must be well thought out and focused. With an explicit and intentional commitment from district leadership, stated again, the four pragmatic, doable elements of successful implementation are:

1. Developing a district guiding coalition and common language

2. Empowering site leadership through staff development and training

3. Monitoring to sustain momentum

4. Ensuring sustainability through ongoing commitment and implementation

These critical components provide a foundation from which district leaders, principals, and teachers can work toward successful PLC implementation. These structures and strategies provide districts with the agility to confront and surmount challenges from support, logistics, and cynics. These structures and strategies are applicable to districts of varying sizes.

Above all, we must never lose focus of our number-one goal: to ensure learning for all. Our efforts to seek the best practices, use data to inform our instructional practices, and ensure learning through a collaborative culture must always be foremost as we move forward.

References and Resources

Archetype. (n.d.). In *Merriam-Webster's online dictionary* (11th ed.). Accessed at www.merriam-webster.com/dictionary/archetype on February 11, 2015.

Aurora West College Preparatory Academy. (n.d.). *Professional learning community rubric*. Accessed at http://awcpa.aurorak12 .org/wp-content/uploads/sites/19/2013/07/Professional -Learning-Community-Rubric.docx on February 26, 2015.

Bean, R. M., Grumet, J. V., & Bulazo, J. (1999). Learning from each other: Collaboration between classroom teachers and reading specialist interns. *Reading Research and Instruction, 38*(4), 273–287.

Buffum, A., Mattos, M., & Weber, C. (2012). *Simplifying response to intervention: Four essential guiding principles*. Bloomington, IN: Solution Tree Press.

Conzemius, A. E., & O'Neill, J. (2014). *The handbook for SMART school teams: Revitalizing best practices for collaboration* (2nd ed.). Bloomington, IN: Solution Tree Press.

Cruz, L. F. (2013, December 18). *Imagined and actual implementation*. Presented in Las Vegas, New Mexico.

Dalmau, T. (2000). *The green line lens*. Accessed at www.dalmau.com /pdfs/green_line_lens.pdf on March 9, 2015.

David, J. L., & Talbert, J. E. (2013). *Turning around a high-poverty district: Learning from Sanger*. San Francisco: S. H. Cowell Foundation.

DuFour, R., DuFour, R., Eaker, R., & Many, T. (2010). *Learning by doing: A handbook for Professional Learning Communities at Work* (2nd ed.). Bloomington, IN: Solution Tree Press.

DuFour, R., & Eaker, R. (1998). *Professional Learning Communities at Work: Best practices for enhancing student achievement.* Bloomington, IN: Solution Tree Press.

DuFour, R., & Fullan, M. (2013). *Cultures built to last: Systemic PLCs at Work.* Bloomington, IN: Solution Tree Press.

DuFour, R., & Marzano, R. J. (2011). *Leaders of learning: How district, school, and classroom leaders improve student achievement.* Bloomington, IN: Solution Tree Press.

Ehren, B. J., Laster, B., & Watts-Taffe, S. (2009). *Creating shared language for collaboration in RTI.* Accessed at http://rtinetwork .org/getstarted/buildsupport/creating-shared-language-for -collaboration-in-rti on January 12, 2015.

Frampton, S., Gil, H., Guastello, S., Kinsey, J., Boudreau-Scott, D., Lepore, M., et al. (2010). *Long-term care improvement guide.* Derby, CT: Planetree.

Fullan, M. (2007). *The new meaning of educational change* (4th ed.). New York: Teachers College Press.

Fullan, M. (2010). *Motion leadership: The skinny on becoming change savvy.* Thousand Oaks, CA: Corwin Press.

Fullan, M. (2011). *The moral imperative realized.* Thousand Oaks, CA: Corwin Press.

Jackson, D., & Temperley, J. (2007). From professional learning community to networked learning community. In L. Stoll & K. S. Louis (Eds.), *Professional learning communities: Divergence, depth and dilemmas* (pp. 45–62). Berkshire, England: Open University Press.

Kotter, J. P. (1996). *Leading change.* Cambridge, MA: Harvard Business School Press.

Kruse, S. D., & Louis, K. S. (2007). Developing collective understanding over time: Reflections on building professional community. In L. Stoll & K. S. Louis (Eds.), *Professional learning communities: Divergence, depth and dilemmas* (pp. 106–118). Berkshire, England: Open University Press.

Marzano, R. J., & Waters, T. (2009). *District leadership that works: Striking the right balance.* Bloomington, IN: Solution Tree Press.

Marzano, R. J., Waters, T., & McNulty, B. A. (2005). *School leadership that works: From research to results.* Alexandria, VA: Association for Supervision and Curriculum Development.

McLaughlin, M. W., & Talbert, J. E. (2006). *Building school-based teacher learning communities: Professional strategies to improve student achievement.* New York: Teachers College Press.

Mehaffey, M. (2001). *Sustaining the momentum: Dancing the dance of collaborative teamwork.* Accessed at http://education.wm.edu /centers/ttac/resources/articles/consultcollaborate /sustainmoment/index.php on January 13, 2015.

School District of Cadott Community. (n.d.). *Possible vision statements.* Accessed at www.cadott.k12.wi.us/blog/MrZBlog /Vision-Mission%20Examples.pdf on January 12, 2015.

Smith, W. R. (2012). Culture of collaboration. *School Administrator, 69*(1), 14–20.

Talbert, J. E. (2010). Professional learning communities at the crossroads: How systems hinder or engender change. In A. Hargreaves, A. Lieberman, M. Fullan, & D. Hopkins (Eds.), *Second international handbook of educational change* (pp. 555–572). New York: Springer.

Walther-Thomas, C., Korinek, L., McLaughlin, V. L., & Williams, B. T. (2000). *Collaboration for inclusive education: Developing successful programs.* Boston: Allyn & Bacon.

Wheatley, M. J. (2006). *Leadership and the new science: Discovering order in a chaotic world* (3rd ed.). San Francisco: Berrett-Koehler.

Williamson, R. M. (2006). *What gets measured gets done: Are you measuring what really matters?* Accessed at http://swspitcrew.com /articles/What%20Gets%20Measured%201106.pdf on January 12, 2015.

Zuieback, S. (2012). *Leadership practices for challenging times: Principles, skills, and processes that work.* Ukiah, CA: Synectics.

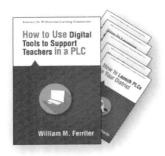

Solutions for Professional Learning Communities

The *Solutions Series* offers practitioners easy-to-implement recommendations on each book's topic—professional learning communities, digital classrooms, or modern learning. In a short, reader-friendly format, these how-to guides equip K–12 educators with the tools they need to take their school or district to the next level.

How to Use Digital Tools to Support Teachers in a PLC
William M. Ferriter
BKF675

How to Leverage PLCs for School Improvement
Sharon V. Kramer
BKF668

How to Coach Leadership in a PLC
Marc Johnson
BKF667

How to Develop PLCs for Singletons and Small Schools
Aaron Hansen
BKF676

How to Cultivate Collaboration in a PLC
Susan K. Sparks and Thomas W. Many
BKF678

How to Launch PLCs in Your District
W. Richard Smith
BKF665

Tremendous, tremendous, tremendous!

The speaker made me do some very deep internal reflection about the **PLC process** and the personal responsibility I have in making the school improvement process work **for ALL kids.**

—Marc Rodriguez, teacher effectiveness coach, Denver Public Schools, Colorado

PD Services

Our experts draw from decades of research and their own experiences to bring you practical strategies for building and sustaining a high-performing PLC. You can choose from a range of customizable services, from a one-day overview to a multiyear process.

Book your PLC PD today!
888.763.9045

Solution Tree